Science Magic

The aim of this book is to stimulate the natural curiosity of young children and encourage them and their parents to make new discoveries.

Through a series of experiments, specially chosen to appeal to 4–8 year olds, basic scientific principles are introduced. How do you make rainbows, play tricks with mirrors, spin paper in the air, make water do things it shouldn't? The drawings are fun and easy to follow, the simple instructions foolproof. At the end of each experiment there is a brief explanation of the science behind it and why it works.

Each experiment in the book can be done using objects and equipment normally found around the house. They have all been tested by the authors and their young children to everyone's satisfaction. They are also safe – no boiling water, no sharp knives, no fire. Some parental guidance and supervision may be necessary however – to explain directions, to help gather materials and to assist in handling equipment. Make learning a fun family adventure.

SCIENCE MAGIC

Scientific Experiments For Young Children

ALISON ALEXANDER and SUSIE BOWER

Illustrated by Carolyn Scrace

Simon and Schuster Books for Young Readers

Published by Simon & Schuster Inc.
New York

Simon and Schuster Books for Young Readers
Simon & Schuster Building
Rockefeller Center
1230 Avenue of the Americas
New York, New York 10020

Published by the Simon & Schuster Juvenile Division
SIMON AND SCHUSTER BOOKS FOR YOUNG READERS
is a trademark of Simon & Schuster Inc.

Manufactured in Hong Kong
Typeset by Columns of Reading, England
Printed in Hong Kong

10 9 8 7 6 5 4 3 2 1
(pbk) 10 9 8 7 6 5 4 3 2 1

Library of Congress Cataloging-in-Publication Data

Alexander, Alison, 1949–

    Science Magic.

    Summary: Illustrated instructions for using easily
available materials in a variety of simple experiments
that introduce basic scientific principles.
    1. Science—Experiments—Juvenile literature.
[1. Science—Experiments   2. Experiments]   I. Bower.
Susie.   II. Scrace. Carolyn, ill.   III. Title.
Q164.A38   1987   507'.8   86–12280
ISBN 0-671-66368-2
ISBN 0-671-66927-3 (pbk)

Contents

Make the Fountain Spout

You will need:

clear plastic screw top bottle
lump of modeling clay
paint or food coloring
hammer and nail
needle
plastic straw
bucket, or saucepan, deep enough to contain whole bottle
hot and cold water

cold
cold

▷ Fill the bottle half way with cold water and add the paint to color. Screw the lid on tightly, and using the hammer and nail, carefully make a hole in it big enough for the straw to fit. Be careful of fingers and thumbs. Ask mom or dad to help.

Push the straw into the hole until it is well below the level of the water. Using the modeling clay, make a seal around the hole and plug the top of the straw. Make a hole in the plug with the needle.

Fill the bucket with hot water. Put the bottle in so that it is well covered with water.

The water in the bottle will start to rise up the straw and spurt out like a fountain.

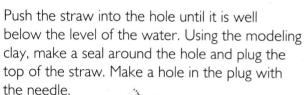

Check you've got enough hot water in the bucket.

The hot water in the bucket warms the air inside the bottle. Hot air needs more space than cold air so the air forces the water out of the way and pushes it up through the straw.

Blow up a Balloon without Using any Breath

You will need:

plastic soda bottle
balloon
felt tip pen
hot and cold water
2 buckets or deep bowls

Put in plenty of water

hot

cold

hot   hot   cold   cold

cold   cold

▷ Blow up the balloon to soften it. Let the air out again.
Fill one bucket with cold water and one with hot. Always be careful with hot water. Fill the bottle half way with cold water. Draw a face on the balloon and fix it over the top of the bottle.
Place the bottle in the hot water bucket so that the water level is right up to the neck of the bottle, and the balloon will pop up. Put it in the cold water bucket and the face will crumple.

Empty cold water out of the bottle and then fill it half way with hot water. Replace the balloon and put the bottle in the cold water bucket. The balloon will be sucked into the bottle. Take it out and place it in the hot water bucket and the balloon will pop up again.

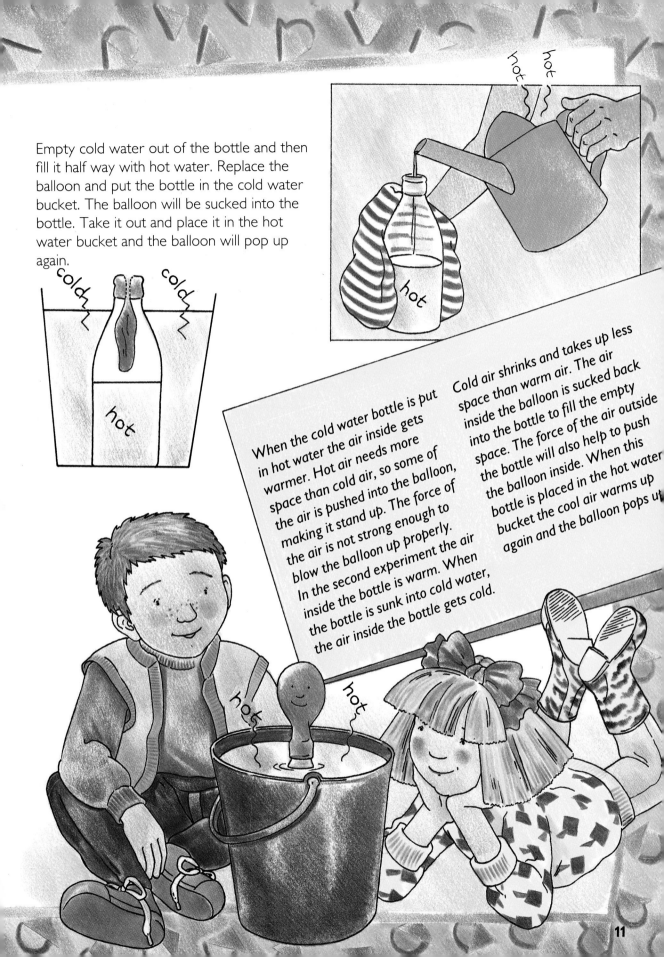

When the cold water bottle is put in hot water the air inside gets warmer. Hot air needs more space than cold air, so some of the air is pushed into the balloon, making it stand up. The force of the air is not strong enough to blow the balloon up properly. In the second experiment the air inside the bottle is warm. When the bottle is sunk into cold water, the air inside the bottle gets cold. Cold air shrinks and takes up less space than warm air. The air inside the balloon is sucked back into the bottle to fill the empty space. The force of the air outside the bottle will also help to push the balloon inside. When this bottle is placed in the hot water bucket the cool air warms up again and the balloon pops up

Water Patterns

You will need:

small empty glass bottle
with a lid
hammer and nail
large glass jar
or bowl
food coloring or paint
(red is best)
hot and cold water

▽
Ask your mom or dad to help
you use the hammer and nail to
make 2 small holes in the lid of
the bottle.

Take the lid off and fill the
bottle with hot water then add
the coloring. Put the lid back
on.

hot

cold

cold

hot hot hot

Fill the large jar or bowl with cold water and submerge the bottle, keeping your finger over the holes until it is in place. (You can lie the bottle on its side if the bowl is not very deep.) Lift off your finger and watch the colored water in the bottle rise up into the cold water and make patterns.

A bottle full of hot water is lighter than a similar bottle full of cold water. This means that the hot water in the bottle will rise up through the cold water, making spiral patterns as it pushes the cold water out of the way.

Spin a Paper Spiral

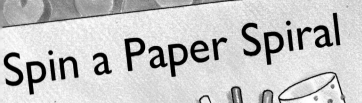

You will need:

paper
scissors
cotton thread
crayons
warm radiator or table lamp
jam jar lid or glass tumbler to
    draw a circle
needle

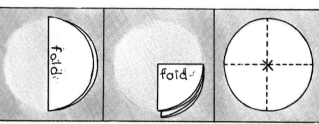

▷ Use the lid or tumbler to draw a circle on the paper and cut it out.

Find the center of the circle by folding the paper in half and then in half again. Open out the circle and the point where the lines cross is the center.

Starting from the center draw a spiral. The lines should be about one half inch (1 cm) apart. You can turn the spiral into a snake or write a message along it, or you can stick foil stars or glitter on the spiral to make a decoration. Then cut it out starting from the outside edge. (Aluminium foil will make a shiny spiral.)

Use the needle to make a small hole through the center point of the spiral. Thread the cotton through and knot it. Fix the spiral so that it hangs a little way above a hot radiator·or lighted table lamp and it will spin round.

The hot air from the radiator is lighter than the cold air around it. The cold air sinks down and pushes the hot air up against the spiral, making it spin.

On a Sunny Day Make a Rainbow

You will need:

mirror
bright sunshine
small mixing bowl (the size
of the bowl will depend on
the size of your mirror)

▽
Fill the bowl half way with water and place it near a window in direct sun.

Hold the mirror in the water at an angle so that the sun shines directly onto it. You will have to move the mirror gently about until the colors of the rainbow begin to appear on the wall.

Lean the mirror against the side of the bowl without disturbing the water too much. When the water stops moving you should be able to see the colors of the rainbow – Red, Orange, Yellow, Green, Blue, Indigo, Violet. As the sun goes behind a cloud the colors will fade.

You can make a rainbow in the garden. Wait until the sun begins to go down and then stand with your back to the sun and spray a shower of water through a hose pipe. As the sun shines on the water drops the colors of the rainbow appear in the spray.

Although you cannot see it, a beam of light is made up from a mixture of all the colors of the rainbow. When the beam hits the water, each color is bent at a different angle. This means the beam of light is split up into separate beams of colored light. The mirror reflects these colors on to the wall where you can see red, orange, yellow, green, blue, indigo, and violet.

If you use a hose, the drops of water from the spray bend the beam of light and split it up into colors in the same way as the water in the bowl does. This forms a rainbow.

Are Colors what they Seem?

You will need:

white blotting paper or filter papers
water-based felt tip pens
jug of water

▽

Using the felt tips, make spots of color
on the blotting paper spacing them quite
far apart.

Put a few drops of water on each color spot and watch to see if they change. When the blotting paper has dried out the colors will show up more clearly.

When ink is dropped on blotting paper it spreads out. The ink in some colored felt tips is made up from a mixture of colors. Some colors spread out further than others so that if the blob of ink is a mixed color you will see the different colors spread out over the blotting paper.

Watch the Colors Disappear

You will need:

colored crayons or paints
scissors
cardboard (cereal packet is fine)

ruler
jam jar lid
large-eyed needle (wool needle is ideal)
length of wool about 3 feet (1 meter) long

Draw a circle on the cardboard using the jam jar lid and cut it out.

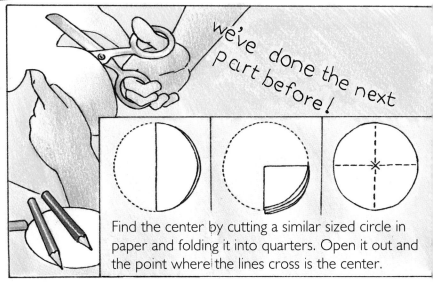

we've done the next part before!

Find the center by cutting a similar sized circle in paper and folding it into quarters. Open it out and the point where the lines cross is the center.

Mark the center of the cardboard circle. Divide the circle into six parts and color each section differently using colors of the rainbow – red, orange, yellow, green, blue, violet. You can color the sections using just red, blue, green, red, blue, green.

With the needle or the point of the scissors make two small holes either side of the center of the circle, one half inch (1 cm) apart. Thread the wool through both holes and knot the ends together to make a loop.

Put one finger in each loop and twist up the wool by spinning your hands round. By moving your hands together and apart again you can make the disc spin. All the colors will disappear as the disc spins and it will look as though it is white.

When the disc is spinning, all the colors go round very fast. You see them all at the same time and your eyes cannot see each different color separately. So you think the disc has no color at all and to your eyes it looks white.

Make a Kaleidoscope

You will need:

2 handbag mirrors the same size
  (oblong are best)
a piece of cardboard the same size as
  the mirrors
greaseproof paper
plastic wrap
Cellophane tape
scissors
small shapes of colored paper, beads,
  tin foil, or other tiny objects

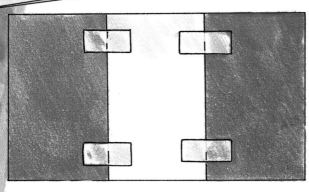

▷ Lay the cardboard on the table and place the mirrors face down on either side of it. Tape them all together.

Turn over the mirrors and cardboard and bend the mirrors together to make a triangle, so that the mirrors are inside the triangle. Tape them together.

Tape the greaseproof paper tightly across one end of the kaleidoscope.

not too many!

Put a few small pieces of colored paper into the kaleidoscope.

Stretch a piece of plastic wrap across the opening to stop the paper bits falling out.

Look down into the kaleidoscope and watch the patterns change as you shake it.

When you look down the kaleidoscope you can see the bits of paper you put in and six different reflections of them. The mirrors and the cardboard are all exactly the same size and when fixed together make a triangle. Because the mirrors are joined in this way they can make many reflections which form a circle of pictures.

Peek Around the Corner with a Periscope

You will need:

nail scissors
2 handbag mirrors (square ones are best)
ruler
oblong cracker box
Cellophane tape
pencil

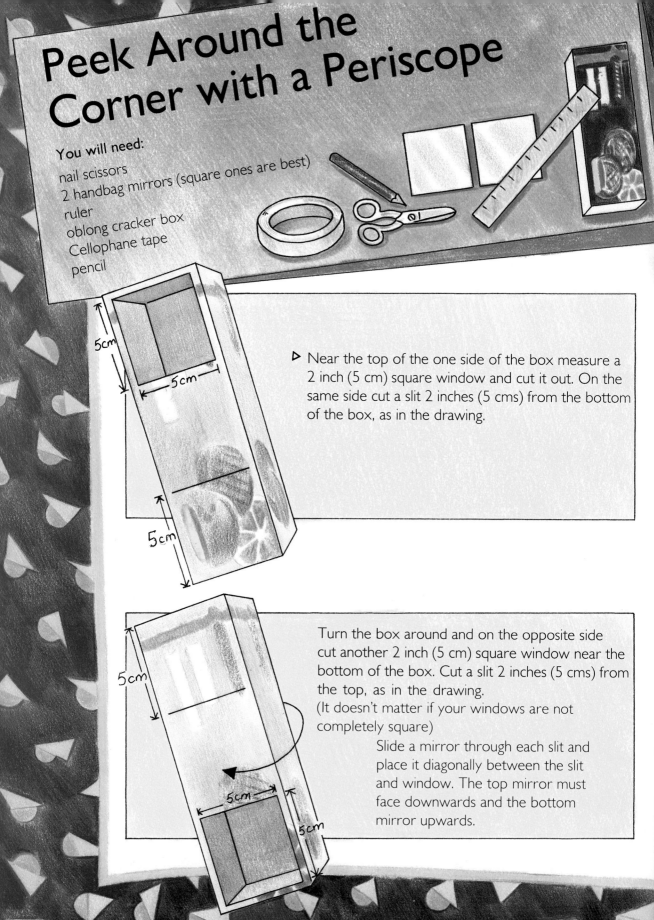

5cm
5cm
5cm

▷ Near the top of the one side of the box measure a 2 inch (5 cm) square window and cut it out. On the same side cut a slit 2 inches (5 cms) from the bottom of the box, as in the drawing.

5cm
5cm
5cm

Turn the box around and on the opposite side cut another 2 inch (5 cm) square window near the bottom of the box. Cut a slit 2 inches (5 cms) from the top, as in the drawing.
(It doesn't matter if your windows are not completely square)

Slide a mirror through each slit and place it diagonally between the slit and window. The top mirror must face downwards and the bottom mirror upwards.

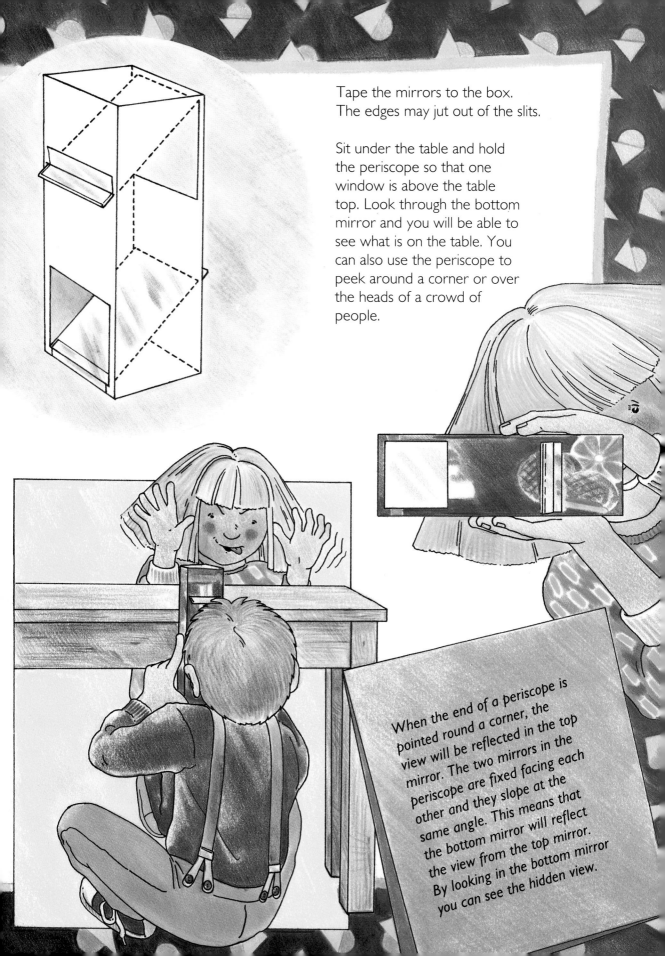

Tape the mirrors to the box. The edges may jut out of the slits.

Sit under the table and hold the periscope so that one window is above the table top. Look through the bottom mirror and you will be able to see what is on the table. You can also use the periscope to peek around a corner or over the heads of a crowd of people.

When the end of a periscope is pointed round a corner, the view will be reflected in the top mirror. The two mirrors in the periscope are fixed facing each other and they slope at the same angle. This means that the bottom mirror will reflect the view from the top mirror. By looking in the bottom mirror you can see the hidden view.

Acrobatic Pictures

You will need:
a small notebook or some sheets of paper folded up to make a booklet
pencils

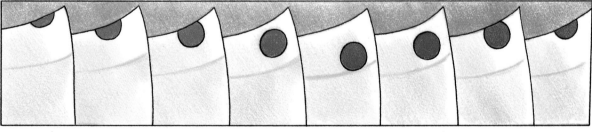

▷ In the top right hand corner of each page, draw a ball, changing its position a little every time.

Bend the corner of the book back and flick the pages. The ball will bounce up and down on the page.

You can turn the ball into a face with sad and happy expressions. You can also draw pin men jumping up and down. But you must remember to change the picture slightly each time.

The pictures flick past your eyes too quickly to see them separately. As the ball is in a slightly different position in each picture it appears as if the ball is bouncing up and down.

Shadow Shapes

You will need:

flashlight
dark room
white paper

▽
Draw the curtains and make the room dark. Turn on the flashlight and place it so that it points towards a plain wall or white sheet of paper.

Hold your hand about two feet in front of the light and it will make a good shadow. As you make different shapes with your hands and move your fingers about, you will see shadow pictures.

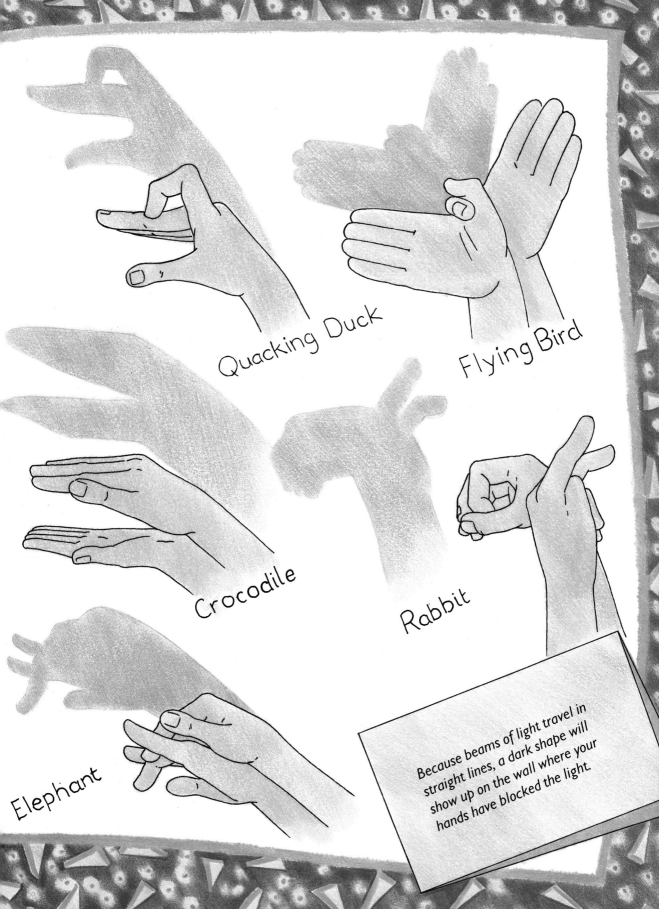

Quacking Duck

Flying Bird

Crocodile

Rabbit

Elephant

Because beams of light travel in straight lines, a dark shape will show up on the wall where your hands have blocked the light.

Stop the Shower without Turning it off

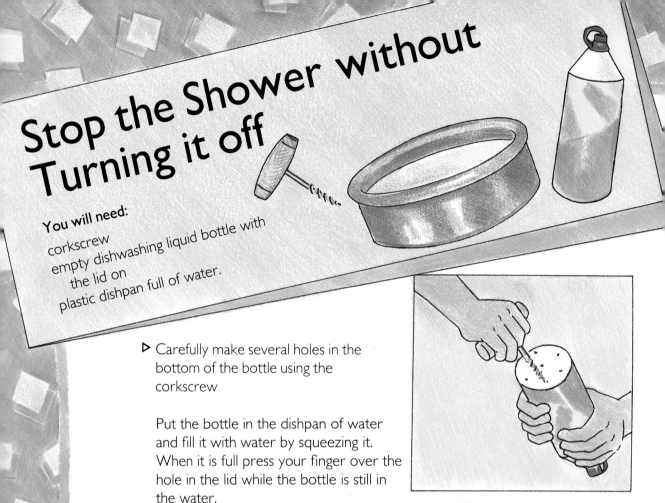

You will need:

corkscrew
empty dishwashing liquid bottle with
  the lid on
plastic dishpan full of water.

▷ Carefully make several holes in the bottom of the bottle using the corkscrew

Put the bottle in the dishpan of water and fill it with water by squeezing it. When it is full press your finger over the hole in the lid while the bottle is still in the water.

Keeping your finger pressed over the hole, lift the bottle out of the water.

Take your finger away and the water comes out of the holes. Press your finger back over the hole and the shower stops.

Although you cannot feel it, the air all around us pushes against anything it touches. There is also a force which pulls all objects towards the earth. This is called gravity. The gravity and the force of the air pushing down on the water are stronger than the air that pushes up against the shower holes. So the water sprays out. When you block the hole in the lid with your finger, you stop the air pushing down on the water. Now the air pushing up is stronger than the gravity pulling down. The shower stops.

Carry Water in a Straw

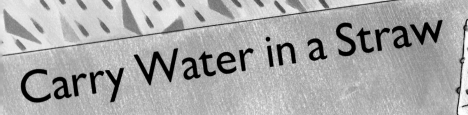

You will need:

straw
glass of water

▽

Suck the water up the straw and when it is full press your finger, or tongue if it is easier, over the top of the straw.

Keeping your tongue or finger over the straw, lift it out of the water. No water will come out. Take your finger away and the water will fall out.

The water is stopped from coming out of the straw for the same reason that the shower you made before stops when you block the hole in the lid. You stop the force of the air pushing it out.

Turn a Glass of Water upside down

You will need:

jug of water
glass tumbler
plastic dishpan
piece of stiff cardboard

▷ Hold the glass over the dishpan and fill it to the brim with water.

Gently slide the cardboard across the surface.

Pressing on the cardboard with one hand, turn the glass upside down. It is best to do this over the dishpan.

Take your hand away from the cardboard and it will stay stuck to the glass.

presto!

The force of air pushing up is stronger than the pull of gravity down. The air presses the card against the glass so strongly that the water cannot come out.

Watch the Milk Erupt

You will need:

milk
food coloring
cereal bowl
dishwashing liquid

▽
Pour the milk into the dish.
Add a few drops of different
food coloring.

Put a drop of dishwashing
liquid on each color and
watch the colors move
around.

Although you cannot see it, milk contains drops of fat which do not mix with the watery food coloring. Wherever the dishwashing liquid touches the drops of fat milk it breaks up the drops of fat milk it breaks up the drops which then spread out, allowing the food coloring and milk to mix.

Amazing!

Marbling

You will need:

tablespoon, teaspoon
cooking oil
food coloring or inks
mixing cup
fork
plain paper (painting book paper is best)
flat roasting pan of cold water

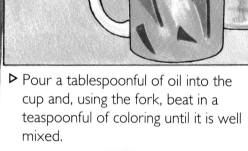

▷ Pour a tablespoonful of oil into the cup and, using the fork, beat in a teaspoonful of coloring until it is well mixed.

Pour the oil and coloring mixture onto the water so that it forms small pools on the surface.
Take a sheet of paper and lay it over the dish for about half a minute, pressing it gently onto the surface of the water if necessary. Lift the paper off. The surface will have a marbled pattern on it. You can also gently rock the paper up and down so that the colors run over the pattern. Add more oil with another color to get a different effect.

If you look in the dish you will see the color bubbles trapped inside the oil pools gradually erupt into the water. You can go on adding oil and colors for as long as you like.

Oil and water will not mix. The explosions of color are caused by the food coloring, which is water based, escaping from the oil drops to mix with the water.

A Word in your Ear

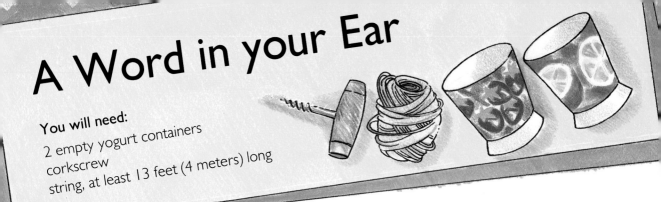

You will need:
2 empty yogurt containers
corkscrew
string, at least 13 feet (4 meters) long

▽
Make a small hole in the bottom of each
yogurt container.

Thread the ends of the string through
the holes in the containers and tie a
knot at each end to stop it slipping out.

~ *Make sure that
the knot is big enough!*

Knock knock

Pull the string taut – you will have to go into different rooms or even up stairs to do this. One person speaks into her yogurt container while the person at the other end places his to his ear and listens to the message.

When you talk the air in the yogurt container vibrates. The string carries these vibrations to the second yogurt container and you hear them as sounds.

Musical Chimes

You will need:
8 glass bottles the same size and shape, and some bottles of varying sizes (soda bottles, sauce bottles, wine bottles, milk bottles — you can also use glass tumblers)
wooden spoon
water

Line the bottles up in order starting with the fullest one. Make sure that they are close together but not touching. Then go along the row tapping each bottle with the wooden spoon below the water line. You will hear the notes getting higher as you tap. You will have to tap milk bottles quite hard.

40

To make a musical scale, take the 8 bottles that are the same size and shape. Pour water up to about 2½ inches (6 cms) into the first bottle. Pour water into all the others so that each has a little more than the bottle next to it.

Fill the odd-sized bottles up to different levels and see which ones make the best sound. Hold one of the bottles close to your mouth and blow over the top. Then try blowing over an empty bottle.

Sounds are made when air vibrates and makes your eardrums vibrate. The faster the vibration, the higher the sound. When you tap one of the bottles the water vibrates. These vibrations travel through the air above to your ear and you hear them as sounds. The deeper the water in the bottle, the lower the note you will hear.

When you blow across the bottle top, the air above the water vibrates. The deeper the air in the bottle, the lower the note you hear.

Play in a Band

Guitar

You will need:

family-sized plastic ice cream carton
assorted elastic bands

Stretch the elastic bands over the ice cream carton and pluck them. If you pull the sides of the carton apart as you pluck, you will hear the sounds change.

Drum

You will need:

balloon, an old popped one will do
rigid container such as a mug or jar

If you are using a new balloon blow it up first to make it more supple and cut the end off so that you can stretch it over the top of the mug. The balloon will stick by itself. Then bang the top with your fingers or a pencil. You can make a louder noise by pinching out the surface of the drum and letting it go.

Whistles

You will need:

scissors   straws

Cut the straws into different lengths. Then at one end of each cut a point. Flatten the straws at the pointed ends — if they are plastic, use your teeth. Put the pointed end of one of the straws in your mouth and blow very hard. Each straw will make a different sound.

tooooooot

Xylophone

You will need:

2 towels
wooden spoon
pieces of wood of different lengths,
    wood that is 1 inch (2 cm) thick is best.

Fold the towels lengthwise to make thick oblong pads and lay them parallel about 4 inches (10 cm) apart.

Rest the pieces of wood across the towels and tap them firmly down the middle with the wooden spoon.

Castanets

You will need:

2 metal spoons the same size

Hold the spoons by their handles, one between your thumb and first finger and the other between your first finger and middle finger. Make sure the backs of the spoons are together, then bang them up and down against the palm of your other hand.

Thumb Piano

You will need:

rulers (wooden ones are best)
heavy books

Place the books at the edge of the table, then push the rulers underneath them so that each one sticks out by a different amount. Flick the ends of the rulers with your thumb and they will make different noises. You must press down hard on the books with your other hand to keep the rulers firmly in place.

Play in a Band

Each instrument makes sounds because something is vibrating. The elastic bands vibrate over the carton, the balloon vibrates over the mug, the pointed ends of the straw vibrate in your mouth, the wood vibrates when it is tapped, the spoons vibrate when they collide, the parts of the rulers that jut out vibrate when pressed.

These vibrations travel through the air to your ear. The different sounds which you hear are produced by the different types of vibrations.